The United Arab Emirates (UAE): Issues for U.S. Policy

Kenneth Katzman

Specialist in Middle Eastern Affairs

January 2, 2014

Congressional Research Service

7-5700

www.crs.gov

RS21852

CRS Report for Congress
Prepared for Members and Committees of Congress

Summary

The UAE's relatively open borders and economy have won praise from advocates of expanded freedoms in the Middle East, but have also produced financial excesses, social ills such as human trafficking, and opportunity for UAE-based Iranian businesses to try to circumvent international sanctions. The social and economic freedoms have not translated into significant political change; the UAE government remains under the control of a small circle of leaders who allow citizen participation primarily through traditional methods of consensus-building. To date, these mechanisms, economic wealth, and reverence for established leaders have enabled the UAE to avoid wide-scale popular unrest. Since 2006, the government has increased formal popular participation in governance through a public selection process for half the membership of its consultative body, the Federal National Council (FNC). But, particularly since the Arab uprisings that began in 2011, there has been increased domestic criticism of the unchallenged power and privileges of the UAE ruling elite. The leadership has resisted any dramatic or rapid further opening of the political process and has suppressed Muslim Brotherhood-linked Islamists and secular opposition activists, drawing substantial criticism from human rights groups.

The UAE has been a significant U.S. partner in efforts to contain Iranian power. A 1994 U.S.-UAE defense cooperation agreement (DCA) provides for U.S. military use of several UAE facilities, and about 5,000 U.S. military personnel are in the UAE, located at those facilities. The UAE was the first Gulf state to order the most sophisticated missile defense system sold by the United States, demonstrating its support for U.S. efforts to assemble a regional missile defense network against Iran's missile force. The UAE has implemented significant financial and economic sanctions against Iran, but it has also maintained trade and commercial ties with Iran in part to avoid antagonizing that large neighbor and avoid the departure of the large number of Iranian businesses in UAE. This UAE-Iran trade, which includes the reexportation of U.S. products to Iran, has sometimes led to incidents of leakage of U.S. and other advanced technologies to Iran. These concerns were underscored by initial dissatisfaction among some Members of Congress with a 2009 U.S.-UAE civilian nuclear cooperation agreement. The UAE has publicly supported the November 24, 2013, interim nuclear agreement between Iran and the international community as potentially lowering regional tensions and has used that possible breakthrough to try to resolve outstanding disputes with Iran. There are no indications the UAE plans to reduce its defense cooperation with the United States as a consequence of the Iran nuclear deal, although reported UAE worries about a potential lessening of the U.S. attention to the Gulf region are prompting it to back greater defense cooperation among the Gulf Cooperation Council (GCC) states.

On other foreign policy issues, the UAE has become increasingly assertive in recent years to try to achieve regional stability, using primarily its ample financial resources. The UAE has deployed about 250 troops to Afghanistan since 2003 and pledges to keep some forces there after the existing international security mission there ends in 2014. In 2011, it sent 500 police to help fellow Gulf Cooperation Council (GCC) state Bahrain confront a major uprising by its Shiite majority; UAE pilots flew combat missions against Muammar Qadhafi of Libya; and the UAE joined the GCC diplomatic effort that brokered a political solution to the unrest in Yemen. The UAE is financially backing armed rebels in Syria, and it is giving substantial aid to the transitional government of Egypt that followed the military ousting of President Mohammad Morsi, a Muslim Brotherhood leader. The UAE also donates large amounts of international humanitarian and development aid, for example for relief efforts in Somalia and for the Palestinians.

Contents

Figures

Tables

Contacts

Governance, Human Rights, and Reform[1]

The United Arab Emirates (UAE) is a federation of seven emirates (principalities): Abu Dhabi, the oil-rich capital of the federation; Dubai, its free-trading commercial hub; and the five smaller and less wealthy emirates of Sharjah, Ajman, Fujayrah, Umm al-Qaywayn, and Ras al-Khaymah. Sharjah and Ras al-Khaymah have a common ruling family—leaders of the Al Qawasim tribe. After Britain announced in 1968 that it would no longer ensure security in the Gulf, six "Trucial States" decided to form the UAE federation in December 1971; Ras al-Khaymah joined in 1972. The UAE federation has completed a major leadership transition since the death of its key founder, Shaykh Zayid bin Sultan Al Nuhayyan, long-time ruler of Abu Dhabi and UAE president, on November 2, 2004.

Shaykh Zayid's first son, Shaykh Khalifa bin Zayid al-Nuhayyan, born in 1948, was at that time Crown Prince and was named ruler of Abu Dhabi upon Zayid's death. In keeping with tradition, although not formal law, Khalifa was subsequently selected as UAE president by the leaders of all seven emirates who comprise the "Federal Supreme Council." The ruler of Dubai traditionally serves concurrently as Vice President and Prime Minister of the UAE; that position has been held by Shaykh Mohammad bin Rashid Al Maktum, architect of Dubai's modernization drive, since the death of his elder brother Shaykh Maktum bin Rashid Al Maktum in January 2006. Shaykh Mohammad bin Rashid also continued as federation Defense Minister. At its review of senior leadership posts on November 3, 2009, the Federal Supreme Council decided that Shaykh Khalifa and Shaykh Mohammad would serve another five-year term. The review was mostly a formality; in practice, the leadership posts change only in the event of death of an incumbent. The Federal Supreme Council meets four times per year to establish general policy guidelines, although the leaders of the seven emirates consult frequently with each other.

Among the heirs apparent, the third son of Zayid, Shaykh Mohammad bin Zayid al-Nuhayyan, born in 1961, is Abu Dhabi crown prince. UAE President Shaykh Khalifa, his elder half-brother, has delegated significant day-to-day governing responsibilities to him, and several members of the UAE cabinet are Shaykh Mohammad bin Zayid's allies. Shaykh Mohammad is also close to one of his full brothers, Shaykh Hazza bin Zayid Al Nuhayyan, who is national security adviser of the UAE federation. Another full brother, Abdullah bin Zayid, is Foreign Minister. The crown prince of Dubai is Shaykh Mohammad bin Rashid's son, Hamdan bin Mohammad Al Maktum, who heads the "Dubai Executive Committee," the equivalent of a cabinet for Dubai emirate. Under a Dubai-level reorganization announced in January 2010, five committees were set up to advise the Executive Committee on major issues.

---

[1] Much of this section is from the State Department's country report on human rights practices for 2012 (released April 19, 2013), http://www.state.gov/j/drl/rls/hrrpt/humanrightsreport/index htm?year=2012&dlid=204370#wrapper; the *International Religious Freedom Report* for 2012 (May 20, 2013), http://www.state.gov/j/drl/rls/irf/religiousfreedom/ index htm?year=2012&dlid=208398#wrapper; and the *Trafficking in Persons Report for 2013* (June 19, 2013), http://www.state.gov/documents/organization/210740.pdf.

Table 1. Some Basic Facts About the UAE

Population	5.47 million, of whom about 1 million (about 20%) are citizens.
Religions	96% Muslim, of whom 16% are Shiite; 4% Christian and Hindu
Ethnic Groups	19% Emirati (citizenry); 23% other Arab and Iranian; 50% South Asian; 8% Western and other Asian expatriate
Size of Armed Forces	About 50,000
Inflation Rate (2013)	About 1.1%
GDP Growth Rate for 2013	4% estimated by IMF
GDP (purchasing power parity, ppp, 2012)	$275 billion. Per capita is $49,800 ppp
Oil Exports	About 2.7 million barrels per day
Foreign Exchange and Gold Reserves	About $67 billion, but some estimates of the value of its sovereign wealth fund investments run into the several hundreds of billions of dollars.
U.S. Exports to the UAE (2012)	$22.5 billion, making UAE the largest U.S. export market in the Arab world and a 50% increase over 2011. Goods sold to UAE are mostly machinery, commercial aircraft, industrial materials, and other high value items.
Imports from UAE by the United States (2012)	$2.25 billion. Less than 10% of that amount was crude oil.
U.S. citizens resident in UAE	About 60,000
Major Projects	Dubai inaugurated "Burj Khalifa," world's tallest building, on January 4, 2010. Burj al-Arab hotel in Dubai bills itself as "world's only 7-star hotel." Abu Dhabi has built local branches of Guggenheim and Louvre museums.

Sources: CIA, *The World Factbook*; U.S. Census Bureau, Foreign Trade Statistics.

The leaders of the other individual emirates are Dr. Sultan bin Muhammad Al Qassimi (Sharjah); Saud bin Saqr Al Qassimi, (Ras al-Khaymah, see below); Humaid bin Rashid Al Nuaimi (Ajman); Hamad bin Muhammad Al Sharqi (Fujayrah); and Saud bin Rashid Al-Mu'alla (Umm al-Qaywayn). Shaykh Saud of Umm al-Qaywayn, who is about 64 years old, was named leader of that emirate in January 2009 upon the death of his father, Shaykh Rashid Al-Mu'alla. These five emirates, often called the "northern emirates," tend to be more politically and religiously conservative and homogenous than are Abu Dhabi and Dubai, which are urban amalgams populated by many Arab, South Asian, and European expatriates.

In Ras al-Khaymah, there was a brief leadership struggle upon the October 27, 2010, death of the ailing longtime ruler, Shaykh Saqr bin Mohammad Al Qassim. He was succeeded by Shaykh Saud bin Saqr, who had been crown prince/heir apparent since 2003, when the ruler removed Saud's elder brother, Shaykh Khalid bin Saqr, from that position. During 2003-2010, using public relations campaigns in the United States and elsewhere, Shaykh Khalid claimed to remain as heir apparent even though the UAE federal government had repeatedly stated that his removal from that position was legitimate and that he held no official position in the UAE. Shaykh Khalid's home in Ras al-Khaymah was surrounded by security forces the night Shaykh Saqr died, enforcing the succession of Shaykh Saud.

Figure 1. Map of United Arab Emirates

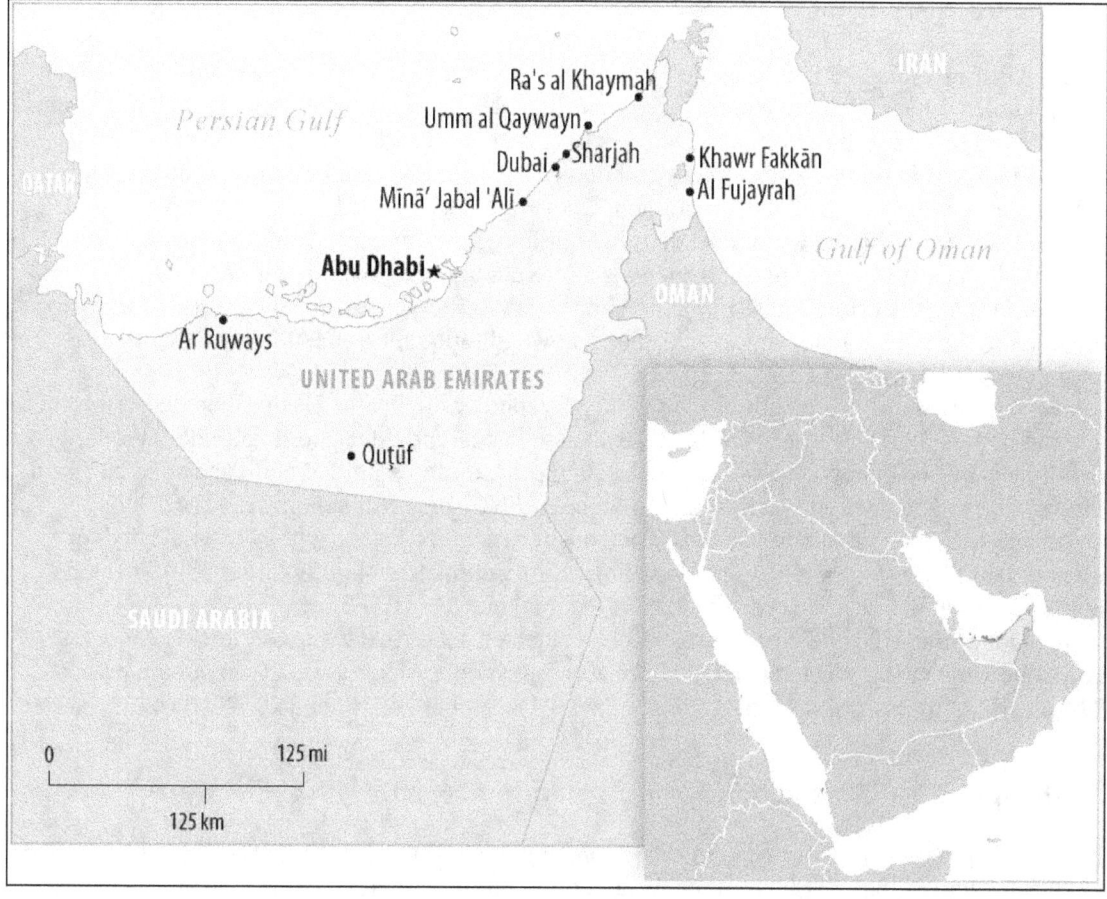

Source: CRS Graphics.

Political Reform and Responses to Opposition

The UAE is not considered by any U.S. or outside organization to be a democracy, but its perceived social openness, coupled with ample wealth that is distributed throughout the citizenry, have long rendered the bulk of the population unwilling to challenge the political system. Prior to an increase in youth and intellectual-led activism in the UAE inspired by the Arab uprisings of 2011, there were few, if any, signs of clamor for more rapid political reform. A combination of modest reforms, repressive measures, and distribution of largesse have enabled the UAE government to avoid significant public unrest that confronted many other governments since the Arab uprisings of 2011. The government has moved against underground activism using arrests, prosecutions, and monitoring of the Internet and social media.

A Top-Driven Modest Reform Process

UAE leaders long argued that Western-style democracy, including elections for the country's leadership, is not needed in UAE because Emiratis are able to express their concerns directly to the leadership through traditional consultative mechanisms. Most prominent among these channels are the open *majlis* (councils) held by many UAE leaders. UAE leaders maintain that Western-style political parties and elections for a legislature or other representative body would inevitably aggravate long dormant schisms among tribes and clans and potentially cause Islamist factions to become radical.

The UAE leadership had long provided a modest measure of popular representation through an all-appointed 40-seat Federal National Council (FNC). The seat distribution of the FNC remains weighted in favor of Abu Dhabi and Dubai, which each hold eight seats. Sharjah and Ras al-Khaymah have six each, and the others each have four. The FNC can review, but not enact or veto, federal legislation, and the government frequently accepts the FNC's legislative recommendations. The FNC can question, but not impeach, ministers. It has conducted such "grillings," mostly on economic and social issues, although the government prohibited the FNC from discussing the economic ramifications of the 2008-2009 global financial crisis. Its sessions are open to the public. Each emirate also has its own all-appointed consultative council.

Leadership resistance to elections to the FNC prevailed until 2006 as electoral processes began to expand in the other Gulf states. The UAE leadership apparently decided it had fallen too far behind its Gulf neighbors and, in December 2006, it instituted a limited and controlled electoral process for half of the FNC seats, with the other 20 FNC seats still appointive. The 2006 electorate was to be limited to about 100 persons for each FNC seat, appointed or elected, or about 4,000 total electors. The Election Commission approved a slightly larger 6,595-person electorate, or about 160 persons per seat. Of the total electors, 1,162 were women (less than 20%). Out of the 452 candidates for the 20 FNC elected seats, there were 65 female candidates. Only one woman was elected (from Abu Dhabi), but another seven were given appointed seats. The election process was spread over three days—December 16, 18, and 20, 2006.

Arab Uprisings Increase Focus on September 24, 2011, FNC Election

Perhaps inspired by the 2011 Arab uprisings and dissatisfied with the slow pace of reform, some UAE intellectuals, businessmen, students, and other groups began agitating peacefully—primarily through written editorials and Internet postings—for more political space. Some UAE youth, on social networking outlets such as Facebook and Twitter, called for a protest on March 25, 2011. It did not produce a significant demonstration in part because the UAE government blocked some social media sites, although most experts attributed the low turnout to insufficient public support for an open challenge to the regime.

Still, the government decided it needed to take more significant steps to address growing reform demands, and it used the opportunity of the September 24, 2011 FNC election to do so. On March 8, 2011, the government expanded the size of the electorate to more than 300 times the total number of FNC seats—a total of 129,000 electors, or "voters"—for the FNC election process. A total of 468 candidates filed to run for the 20 seats up for election on September 24, 2011, including 85 women—little more than the number of candidates who filed to run in the 2006 process. However, the 2011 electorate was nearly half female, in contrast to the fewer than 20% electors in the 2006 process. There was a ruling that no candidate spend more than about $545,000 on their campaigns.

There was widespread press reporting of citizen apathy about the election, with little information about the election or campaigns in the media, little evidence of any campaigning, and reportedly little enthusiasm. Turnout averaged about 25%, which UAE officials called disappointing, and which was apparently pulled down by the 21% turnout in the largest emirate, Abu Dhabi.

Of the 20 winners, only one was female (Sheika Isa Ghanem); she is from Umm Al Quwain, one of the more conservative emirates. It was believed that female candidates would have the best chance of winning in Dubai, considered the most liberal of the emirates. Other winners were elected along tribal lines; in Abu Dhabi, three of the four who were elected are from the Al Amiri tribe. The FNC as a whole—the election winners and the other twenty to be appointed—began their sessions in mid-November. Of those appointed, six were women, bringing the total number of women in the FNC to seven. Upon the FNC's convening, the government selected one of the appointed members, well-known writer Mohammad al-Murr, as Speaker. A woman and another appointed member (of the eight appointed women), Amal al-Qubaisi, was selected deputy speaker, making her the first women to hold so high a position in any GCC legislative body.

However, insisting on implementing political opening at a gradual pace, the government has not implemented calls—such as a March 2011 petition, signed by 160 UAE intellectuals—to transform the FNC into a fully elected body with powers similar to those of a Western-style parliament.[2] Nor is the leadership apparently willing to allow formal political parties. Minister of State for FNC Affairs Anwar Gargash wrote in a UAE paper (*The National*) on August 26, 2012, that "The UAE's end goal is not a liberal multiparty system. This model does not correspond with our cultural or historical development."[3] His comments came following an August 1, 2012, announcement by several Islamists of the formation of a political party called "Al Umma"—an alleged violation of UAE laws that do not grant citizen rights to form political parties.

Accommodation and Pressure on Liberal, Pro-Democracy Activists

As an alternative to expanding the FNC's powers, the government has attempted to address growing youth activism and other popular demands. In March 2011, the government announced investment of about $1.5 billion in utilities infrastructure of the poorer, northern emirates. It also raised military pensions by 70% and introduced subsidies for some foodstuffs. To prevent Internet and underground agitation from turning to large public demonstrations, authorities generally disperse protests and public gatherings that are political in nature, unless such gatherings align with government policies. On March 12, 2013, the government announced a minor cabinet reshuffle—advertised as a "new look" to bring in youthful figures and ideas. The relatively young and dynamic Suhail al-Mazroui was appointed Energy Minister. An Abu Dhabi royal family member, Shaykh Abdullah bin Mubarak al-Nuhayyan, was moved to head a newly formulated Ministry of Culture, Youth and Social Development, with expanded powers to reach out to UAE youth. The government's most prominent female minister, Minister of Foreign Trade Shaykha Lubna Al Qassimi, was given a more prominent role as head of a new Ministry of Development and International Cooperation, which is in charge of all UAE foreign aid and cooperation with international bodies.

The government also has suppressed underground political activism by Islamists as well as by pro-democracy liberals. On April 8, 2011, a prominent Dubai blogger and activist, Ahmad Mansour Al Shehi, was arrested; his detention came two months after another activist made a speech in Sharjah emirate in support of Egyptian protesters. Four other critics and online activists were arrested later in April 2011 and charged with violating a provision of the penal code that prevents publicly humiliating senior officials. The so-called "UAE-5" appeared in court on June

---

[2] Al Jazeera News Network, March 9, 2011.

[3] Anwar Gargash. "Amid Challenges, UAE Policies Engage Gradual Reforms." *The National*, August 26, 2012.

15 and October 2, 2011. Human rights organizations said their trials violated the most basic rights of the accused, and called on UAE leaders to release the five. Those calls were heeded on November 28, 2011, when President Khalifa commuted the "UAE-5" jail sentences that had been announced the previous day.

During April and May 2011, the government dissolved the elected board of directors of the Jurist Association and the Teachers Association, leading civil society groups, after members of their boards signed petitions for political reforms. The boards were reconstituted with government appointees. The Jurists' Association's Human Rights Committee and the Emirates Human Rights Association (EHRA) are the only two recognized local human rights organizations in the country.

Efforts Against Islamists

A long-term potential source of domestic opposition are Islamist movements linked to the Muslim Brotherhood. These movements have been generally nonviolent and limited their activities to social and relief work. However, possibly perceiving that Islamist movements have gained strength regionally after Muslim Brotherhood member Mohammad Morsi came to power in Egypt in 2012, the government has been arresting members of a Brotherhood-affiliated Islamist group, Islah (Reform). The government might also fear that Islamist groups in UAE could join with secular activists to mount a major challenge to the government, as happened in Egypt in 2011. Islah is one of the oldest and best organized groups in the UAE, first appearing in UAE in 1974, and has its base of support in the poorer and more religiously conservative northern emirates. UAE officials have accused Islah and other Muslim Brotherhood affiliates in UAE of obtaining support from the Muslim Brotherhood in Egypt and of having ties to Yusuf Qaradawi, a pro-Brotherhood Egyptian cleric resident in neighboring Gulf state Qatar.[4]

The UAE crackdown on the Brotherhood began in December 2011, when it revoked the citizenship of a Muslim Brotherhood figure who headed an institution called the "Innovative Thinking Center" in Dubai emirate. On April 20, 2012, an Islah member who belongs to the royal family of Ras al-Khaymah, Dr. Sultan al-Qasimi, was arrested. Another, arrested on July 16, 2012, was human rights lawyer Mohammad al-Roken, who has provided legal services not only to Islah but also to the "UAE-5" mentioned above. On November 12, 2012, a UAE court rejected an appeal by seven Islamists against the Interior Ministry's revocation of their citizenship on the grounds of links to terrorist groups.

The government continued to arrest suspected Brotherhood activists throughout 2012. According to the State Department human rights report for 2012, released April 19, 2013, the government arrested a total of 80 persons for suspected Brotherhood activity, of which 12 were Egyptian nationals. On March 4, 2013, a trial began for 94 UAE nationals (those arrested in 2012 and others arrested in 2011 and early 2013) accused of forming a secret Muslim Brotherhood-affiliated network that was plotting a coup against the UAE government. Human rights groups say some of the suspects were tortured and deprived of proper legal representation. On July 2, 2013, the UAE State Security Court sentenced 68 of the 94 to prison terms of between seven and 15 years for "plotting to overthrow the state." The other 26 were acquitted. While that trial was underway, on June 19, 2013, UAE authorities referred another 30 persons, of which 14 are Egyptian nationals, to that court for alleged connections to the Muslim Brotherhood in Egypt. Their trial started on November 5, 2013, but has adjourned several times.

---

[4] "UAE Targets Muslim Brotherhood in Crackdown on Dissent," BBC, September 26, 2012.

International Criticism of UAE Record

On October 26, 2012, the European parliament adopted a resolution criticizing the deteriorating human rights situation; the UAE government claimed the resolution was based on erroneous information brought to the European parliament by UAE bloggers and other activists. Despite that European step, several European governments with close financial or security ties to the UAE, including Italy and France, made statements indicating disagreement with the European parliament resolution. The resolution did not prevent the UAE from assuming a seat on the U.N. Human Rights Council on November 12, 2012.

U.S. Democracy Promotion Efforts and UAE Restrictions

The United States has long sought to promote democracy, rule of law, and civil society in the Persian Gulf region, including in UAE, with relatively small programs and quiet diplomacy. This policy has been implemented through State Department programs to promote student and women's political participation, entrepreneurship, legal reform, civil society, independent media, and international trade law compliance—funded largely by the State Department's Middle East Partnership Initiative (MEPI). These programs are conducted with the knowledge and acquiescence of the UAE government and thereby accomplish the U.S. goal of avoiding injury to the U.S.-UAE security relationship. The U.S. Embassy in Abu Dhabi houses a MEPI office/staff that runs the MEPI programs throughout the Gulf region.

Still, suggesting its sensitivity to activities that could empower domestic opposition groups, the UAE has acted against some U.S.-funded democracy promotion groups. On April 5, 2012, the government closed the National Democratic Institute (NDI) office in Dubai, and briefly barred both its American director and Serbian deputy director from leaving the country. NDI had been working for four years, with license from the UAE government and U.S. funding, to promote women's rights and to advise on municipal governance. The government also shut down the office of the German democracy-promotion organization, the Konrad Adenauer Foundation, which was performing similar work. UAE government representatives continue to insist that NDI and the Adenauer Foundation were meddling in its internal affairs and that such activity was unacceptable. U.S. public criticism of these UAE government actions has been relatively minor and episodic. Official accounts of virtually all high-level U.S.-UAE meetings in 2013 focused almost entirely on regional and security issues, with little if any mention of domestic UAE issues.

General Human Rights-Related Issues

Although the UAE government's reaction to the few acts of opposition discussed above may color future assessments, the State Department human rights report for 2012, released April 19, 2013, was similar to that of previous reports, asserting that there are unverified reports of torture, government restrictions of freedoms of speech and assembly, and lack of judicial independence.[5]

---

[5] http://www.state.gov/j/drl/rls/hrrpt/humanrightsreport/index.htm#wrapper

Press and Research Institute Freedoms

Prior to its efforts to ferret out unrest, the UAE had drawn praise for its free-wheeling media. The post of Information Minister was abolished in 2006 to allow for full media independence. However, in April 2009, a media law drew opposition from some human rights groups who said it allows for penalties against journalists who personally criticize UAE leaders. Provisions governing media licensing do not clearly articulate the standards the government will apply in approving or denying licenses for media organs to operate. The UAE government said the law does not apply to the "Free Zones" in UAE in which major foreign media organizations operate.

Part of the government effort to suppress dissent was a "cybercrimes decree" issued by President Khalifa on November 13, 2012 (Federal Legal Decree No. 5/2012). In issuing the decree, the government established a legal base to prosecute and jail people who use information technology to agitate against the regime or demand more political rights. According to Human Rights Watch, which criticized the decree, Article 28 of the ruling provides for imprisonment and large fines for anyone who uses information technology to incite actions that endanger state security or infringe on the public order. Article 30 provides for life imprisonment for anyone using such technology to advocate the overthrow or change of the system of governance. On December 23, 2013, a UAE court sentenced a U.S. national, Shezanne Cassim, to one year in jail for violating the 2012 cybercrimes decree by making a video parodying youths in Dubai. U.S. diplomats attended the court proceedings.

Since 2010, there have been increasing restrictions on the ability of research institutes to operate. Several such institutes had opened in UAE since the 1990s because of the perceived openness to free expression and ideas. During 2010-2012, the government applied increasingly strict criteria to licensing research institutes and some, such as the Dubai-based Gulf Research Center (GRC), left the UAE entirely. In August 2012, a U.S. academic, Matthew Duffy, had his contract with a UAE university terminated for lectures advocating media and journalistic freedom. In November 2012, the UAE ordered the Rand Corporation to close its office in Abu Dhabi, which was focused on research in education, public safety, and environmental health. UAE officials also have denied entry to some academics and human rights organizations officials who are highly critical of the UAE human rights record.[6]

Justice/Rule of Law

The UAE has a dual court system. Sharia (Islamic law) courts adjudicate criminal and family law matters. Civil courts, based on French and Egyptian legal systems, adjudicate civil law matters. The federal judiciary in the UAE began in 1973 with the establishment of the Federal Supreme Court. The federal judiciary now comprises the Federal Supreme Court, Federal First Instance Courts, and Federal Appeal Courts. The Federal Supreme Court consists of a president and a maximum number of five judges appointed by a decree issued by the President of the UAE and confirmed by the Federal Supreme Council. The Federal Supreme Court looks into matters such as various disputes erupting between the member emirates or between one or more emirate and the UAE federal government, the constitutionality of federal and other laws and legislations, conflicts of jurisdiction between the federal and local judicial authorities in the country, conflict of jurisdiction between the judicial authority in one Emirate and another, and crimes directly affecting the interests of the UAE federation. It also interprets the provisions of the constitution

---

[6] CRS conversations with UAE officials. 2012-2013.

and questioning ministers and senior federal officials for official misconduct. Under the constitution, each emirate has the right to join the federal judiciary system or maintain its own judicial system, and Abu Dhabi, Dubai, and Ras al-Khaymah have opted for the latter arrangement. According to the State Department, foreign nationals hold many positions in the judiciary, making them subject to political influence because they can be deported easily. Furthermore, local rulers review criminal and civil cases before referral to prosecutors, and these political leaders review sentences as well—and the rulers' decisions supersede those of any court.

Some human rights groups express concerned about a 2012 amendment to the UAE consittution that set up a "Federal Judicial Council" chaired by UAE President Khalifa. His deputy on that body is the chair of the Federal Supreme Court, Dr. Abdul Wahab Abdul. UAE officials said the new body was needed to decide on all matters relating to the judicary, judges, and judicial policies and legislation. Human rights groups objected to the fact that the new body is chaired by the UAE President, but the UAE government stressed that the constitutional amendment enshrined judicial independence.

Many observers note that justice in UAE is selective. For example, on January 10, 2010, a UAE court acquitted the UAE president's brother, Shaykh Issa bin Zayid Al Nuhayyan, on charges of torturing an Afghan merchant. He was acquitted even though there was a video available of Shaykh Issa beating the Afghan and driving over his legs with a sport vehicle, and even though three nonroyals involved in the incident were convicted. The UAE court ruled that Shaykh Issa was not liable because he was taking prescription drugs that affected his actions.

The UAE justice system has often come under criticism when expatriates are involved. Even though the UAE promotes itself as a popular tourist destination, Western expatriates have sometimes been arrested for sexual activity on UAE beaches. Arrests of noncitizens increased during the 2008-2009 financial crisis, possibly out of citizen frustration that globalization and dramatic economic expansion have led to bursting of the economic "bubble" in UAE. In 2007, human rights groups criticized the conservative-dominated justice system for threatening to prosecute a 15-year-old French expatriate for homosexuality, a crime in UAE, when he was raped by two UAE men; the UAE men were later sentenced for sexual assault and kidnapping. In 2012, a 78-year-old pediatrician from South Africa, Cyril Karabus, was imprisoned for alleged issues of malpractice related to his six-week service as a doctor in Abu Dhabi in 2002.[7] In July 2013, a Norwegian woman was sentenced to 16 months in jail by a Dubai court for having sex outside marriage after she reported being raped. On July 22, 2013, several days after the sentenced was publicized and drew an outcry from human rights organizations, the woman reported that her case had been dismissed and she was free to leave the UAE.

Women's Rights

Progress on women's political rights has been steady—as exemplified by the November 2011 appointment of a woman as deputy FNC Speaker. Observers say the UAE is perhaps the only country in the Middle East where women are fully accepted working in high-paying professions such as finance and banking. Still, women in the UAE are at a disadvantage in divorce cases and other family law issues. As of December 2011, UAE women are allowed to pass on their citizenship to their children—the first GCC state to allow this.

---

[7] Lydia Polgreen. "Emirates' Laws Trap a Doctor Just Passing Through." *New York Times*, April 12, 2013.

There are four women in the cabinet: Shayha Lubna al-Qassimi (discussed above); Mariam al-Roumi, minister of social affairs; and two ministers without portfolio—Reem al-Hashimi and Maitha al-Shamsi. Seven women are in the Federal National Council, as discussed above, and six women serve on the 40-seat consultative council in Sharjah emirate. About 10% of the UAE diplomatic corps is now female; none served prior to 2001. In September 2013, the UAE appointed a female, Lana Nusseibeh, as UAE Permanent Representative to the United Nations. In November 2008, Dubai emirate appointed 10 female public prosecutors. The UAE Air Force has four female fighter pilots. The percentage of female voters in the September 2011 FNC election process was expanded to nearly 50%, as discussed above.

Religious Freedom

The State Department report on international religious freedom for 2012, issued May 20, 2013, repeated the previous year's assessment that there was no significant change in the government's respect for religious freedom during 2012.[8] The constitution provides for freedom of religion but also declares Islam as the official religion of the country. The death penalty for conversion from Islam remains on the books but is not known to be enforced.

In practice, non-Muslims in UAE are free to practice their religion; there are 35 Christian churches built on land donated by the ruling families of the various emirates, but there are no Jewish synagogues or Buddhist temples. There is a Sikh temple that shares a building with one of two existing Hindu temples. Buddhists, Hindus, Sikhs, and Jews conduct religious ceremonies in private homes, generally without interference.

The Shiite Muslim minority is free to worship and maintain its own mosques, but Shiite mosques receive no government funds and there are no Shiites in top federal posts. At times, the government has acted against non-UAE Shiite Muslims because of their perceived support for Iran, Syrian President Bashar Al Assad, Lebanese Hezbollah, and the mostly Shiite opposition in Bahrain. In 2012, the government closed a Shiite madrassa (school) and, in May 2012, it denied permission to UAE Shiites to host a meeting of worldwide Shiites. In March 2013, the government deported 30 Shiite Muslims, including those from Pakistan, Iraq, Syria, and Lebanon. The UAE and other GCC states are taking steps, including expulsions of Lebanese Shiites, to pressure Lebanese Hezbollah for its direct military support of the beleaguered Assad regime.

Labor Rights

The law prohibits all forms of compulsory labor, but it is not enforced effectively. On several occasions, foreign laborers working on the large, ambitious construction projects in Dubai have conducted strikes to protest poor working conditions and nonpayment of wages. Some of these concerns have been addressed by the Labor Ministry's penalizing of employers, and a process, formulated in June 2008, to have workers' salaries deposited directly in banks.

Human Trafficking

Other social problems might be a result of the relatively open economy of the UAE, particularly in Dubai. The UAE is still considered a "destination country" for women trafficked from Asia and

---

[8] http://www.state.gov/j/drl/rls/irf/religiousfreedom/index.htm?year=2012&dlid=208416#wrapper

the former Soviet Union. The Trafficking in Persons report for 2013 released June 19, 2013, again placed the UAE in "Tier 2"—the same level as in the 2010, 2011, and 2012 reports and an improvement from the "Tier 2: Watch List" placement in 2009. The Tier 2 placement for 2013 was determined, as it was in the prior years, on the grounds that the UAE does not meet the minimum standards for eliminating human trafficking, but is taking significant efforts to do so.

The 2013 report notes that UAE authorities have prosecuted and punished sex trafficking offenders. However, the UAE efforts against forced labor—including unlawful withholding of passports, restrictions on movement, nonpayment of wages, and physical or sexual abuse of workers—have been less clear. The 2013 report states that, for the first time ever, the Ministry of Labor reported statistics on the number of cases of labor complaints it had referred for prosecution, although not every case involved forced labor. An issue in previous years had been trafficking of young boys as camel jockeys, but that issue was largely alleviated with repatriation of many of those trafficked, and the use of robot jockeys at camel races. In October 2013, the UAE government set up a fund to help human trafficking victims rebuild their lives; the funds will be channeled through the Ewa'a organization, in conjunction with the UAE's "National Committee to Combat Human Trafficking." Ewa'a runs shelters in several UAE emirates for trafficking victims.

Foreign Policy and Defense

Following the 1990 Iraqi invasion of Kuwait, the UAE determined that it needed a closer security relationship with the United States. The UAE did not necessarily fear a direct threat from Saddam Hussein's Iraq, which is at the north end of the Persian Gulf, but the UAE saw the United States as the key actor in any successful effort to balance out Iranian power—a primary UAE concern. That cooperation has taken on numerous dimensions, including purchase of advanced missile defense capabilities designed to counter Iranian ballistic missiles, as well as U.S. military deployments intended to demonstrate resolve to Iran. Beyond the Gulf, UAE actions and responses to the 2011-2013 unrest in the Middle East suggest that the UAE is increasingly assertive on foreign policy in an effort to create and preserve regional stability.

UAE cooperation with the United States has not come at the expense of UAE participation in all GCC security and foreign policy coordination forums or mechanisms. And, some Gulf leaders, including those in the UAE, say that the November 24, 2013, interim Iran nuclear deal could cause the United States to de-emphasize Gulf security. U.S. officials, including Defense Secretary Chuck Hagel on a visit to the region in early December 2013, have sought to reassure the Gulf states of the U.S. commitment to their security. Still, the GCC summit in Kuwait during December 10-11, 2013, agreed to a plan, subject to further study, for more intra-GCC cooperation such as a joint military command. The plan was widely seen by experts as an effort by the Gulf leaders to look to the GCC itself for security of the Gulf and perhaps rely less on the United States. The GCC summit decisions also included the establishment of a GCC maritime security coordination center, part of which is to be a new "Gulf Academy for Strategic and Security Studies" to be located in Abu Dhabi.

One obstacle to greater GCC defense cooperation are schisms among some of the GCC states. The UAE's past border disputes and other disagreements with Saudi Arabia occasionally flare. A 1974 "Treaty of Jeddah" with Saudi Arabia formalized Saudi access to the Persian Gulf via a corridor running through UAE, in return for UAE gaining formal control of villages in the Buraymi oasis area. And, the UAE and some of the other smaller Gulf states are wary of ceding too much GCC authority to bloc leader Saudi Arabia, and the UAE and others apparently still prefer to deal with the United States bilaterally rather than as a GCC bloc.

Security Cooperation with the United States/Defense Cooperation Agreement (DCA)

The framework for U.S.-UAE defense cooperation is a July 25, 1994, bilateral Defense Cooperation Agreement (DCA), the text of which is classified.[9] The DCA initially was accompanied by a separate "Status of Forces Agreement" (SOFA) giving U.S. military personnel in UAE certain legal immunities, but several incidents caused the UAE to void the SOFA and legal incidents are now handled on a "case-by-case basis." Under the DCA, the UAE has allowed U.S. equipment pre-positioning and U.S. warship visits at its large Jebel Ali port, which is capable of handling aircraft carriers, and it permitted the upgrading of airfields in the UAE that were used for U.S. combat support flights during Operation Iraqi Freedom (OIF) and continued to be used for flights in support of U.S. operations in Afghanistan.[10]

According to UAE and U.S. officials, there are about 5,000 U.S. forces in the UAE—an increase from 2010-2012 levels of about 3,000—up substantially from 800 before OIF. The U.S. forces in UAE are mostly Air Force, deployed primarily at Al Dhafra air base handling KC-10 refueling and several types of surveillance aircraft such as the Global Hawk and the AWACS (Airborne Warning and Control System). Some U.S. personnel reportedly are stationed at naval facilities at Fujairah. In April 2012—possibly to signal additional resolve over Iran's nuclear program—the United States reportedly deployed several "Stealth" F-22 Raptor combat aircraft to Al Dhafra—a deployment that could explain why U.S. forces in UAE have increased since early 2012.[11]

The U.S.-UAE defense pact has also reportedly included U.S. training of UAE armed forces, UAE forces are relatively small—about 51,000—but have benefitted from U.S. and other training. At the Air Warfare Center near Al Dhafra Air Base, UAE and U.S. forces conduct extensive exercises on early warning, air and missile defense, and logistics. The UAE also hosts the Integrated Air Missile Defense Center, a major training facility for Gulf and U.S.-GCC cooperation on missile defense. Since 2009, UAE Air Force personnel have participated in the yearly Desert Falcon exercises at Nellis Air Force Base in Nevada, according to UAE representatives. About 350 UAE military personnel study and train in the United States each year, mostly through the Foreign Military Sales program, through which the UAE buys most of its U.S.-made arms. U.S. military officers say that UAE operators of HAWK surface-to-air missile batteries are on par with U.S. operators of that system and that UAE fighter pilots are "combat ready," as demonstrated in operations in Libya in 2011. Other observers say that USE special operations forces are highly proficient.

The UAE has also looked to private parties to train its forces. The UAE confirmed on May 15, 2011, that it had retained the U.S. private firm Reflex Responses, to provide "operational, planning, and training support," to the UAE military. The statement followed a *New York Times* report that the UAE had hired the firm, which is run by Eric Prince, who founded the Blackwater

---

[9] Some provisions are discussed in Sami Hajjar, *U.S. Military Presence in the Gulf: Challenges and Prospects* (U.S. Army War College: Strategic Studies Institute), March 2002, p. 27.

[10] Jaffe, Greg. "U.S. Rushes to Upgrade Base for Attack Aircraft." *Wall Street Journal*, March 14, 2003.

[11] *Washington Post*, April 28, 2012.

security contractor, to a $529 million contract to build a foreign mercenary battalion to help defend the UAE from internal revolt or related threats.[12] The State Department investigated the reports to determine whether the contract violated any U.S. laws controlling the export of U.S. defense technology and expertise. No findings have been announced. *Defense News* reported on November 25, 2013, that a U.S. firm, Knowledge International, has provided 125 former U.S. Army officers to help improve the organization and performance of UAE land forces.

U.S. and Other Arms Sales

The UAE views arms purchases from the United States as enhancing the U.S. commitment to UAE security, and the United States views the sales as enhancing the U.S.-led Gulf security architecture by building up indigenous GCC capabilities and promoting inter-operability. From 2007 to 2010, the UAE agreed to acquire more U.S. defense articles and services through the Foreign Military Sales program—$10.4 billion worth—than any other country in the world except Saudi Arabia.[13] Until 2008, the most significant buy was the March 2000 purchase of 80 U.S. F-16 aircraft, equipped with the Advanced Medium Range Air to Air Missile (AMRAAM) and the HARM (High Speed Anti-Radiation Missile), a deal exceeding $8 billion. Congress did not try to block the aircraft sale, although some Members questioned the AMRAAM as an introduction of the weapon into the Gulf. Defense industry sources say that the equipment and capabilities on the F-16s sold to the UAE were highly sophisticated. Earlier, in September 2006, the United States sold UAE High Mobility Artillery Rocket Systems (HIMARS) and Army Tactical Missile Systems (ATACMs), valued at about $750 million.

Among more recent major sales:

- In March 2009, the UAE signed agreements with Boeing Co. and Lockheed Martin Corp. to buy $3 billion worth of military transport aircraft (C-17 and C-130, respectively).

- On November 4, 2010, the Defense Security Cooperation Agency (DSCA) notified Congress of two potential sales: $140 million worth of ATACMs and associated support; and a possible $5 billion worth of AH-64 Apache helicopters (30 helicopters, remanufactured to Block III configuration).[14]

- On November 30, 2011, DSCA notified (transmittal number 10-56) a potential sale of 4,900 Joint Direct Attack Munitions (JDAM) kits with an estimated value of $304 million. The widespread perception was that the munitions could potentially be used to strike hard targets, such as nuclear facilities in Iran, although there are no indications the UAE would conduct such a strike on its own. The United States previously sold the UAE JDAM kits worth $326 million in January 3, 2008.

- On April 25, 2013, Secretary of Defense Chuck Hagel, visiting UAE, reportedly finalized a sale to UAE of an additional 25-30 F-16 aircraft and associated "standoff" air-to-ground munitions. The sale was in conjunction with similar weapons sales to Israel and Saudi Arabia, and which Secretary Hagel and other

---

[12] http://www.nytimes.com/2011/05/15/world/middleeast/15prince.html?_r=1&partner=rss&emc=rss.

[13] CRS Report: U.S. Arms Sales: Agreement with and Deliveries to Major Clients, 2003-2010.

[14] DSCA transmittal number 10-52. http://www.dsca.mil.

officials clearly indicated were intended to signal U.S. and partner resolve to Iran.[15] The agreement came about one week after President Obama met visiting Abu Dhabi Crown Prince Shaykh Mohammad bin Zayid at the White House on April 16, 2013. On October 15, 2013, DSCA (transmittal no. 13-48) notified a potential sale of numerous precision-guided missiles for its F-16 fleet, including 20 of the advanced ATM-84 SLAM-ER Telemetry missile and 5,000 GBU-39/B "bunker buster" bombs. (The sale of the SLAM-ER would represent the first sale of that weapon to a Gulf state.) The principal contractors will be Boeing and Raytheon, and the estimated cost of the munitions is $4 billion. Press reports say the UAE and other Gulf states are interested in purchasing the advanced F-35 "Joint Strike Fighter" if and when the United States approves it for sale to the Gulf states.

Possible Drone Sale? At the IDEX defense show in February 2013, the UAE reportedly agreed to a commercial sale, worth about $200 million, for Predator unmanned aerial vehicles (UAVs), although the system apparently would be unarmed and for surveillance only. Still, Defense Department officials say they have not completed formulating a policy for the sale of such equipment to the Gulf states and it is possible that the deal might not be permitted by DOD.

THAAD and Other Major Missile and Air Defense Systems

A key U.S. objective has been to organize an integrated Gulf-wide missile defense network against Iran's missile force, and this objective was a major factor in the formation of the "U.S.-GCC Strategic Cooperation Forum." The Forum held its first meeting on March 31, 2012, with then Secretary of State Clinton attending, in Riyadh, Saudi Arabia. Subsequently, Deputy Assistant Secretary of State Frank Rose spoke in Abu Dhabi on April 12, 2012,[16] on the missile defense issue, saying, "As our partners acquire greater missile defense capabilities, the United States will work to promote interoperability and information sharing among the GCC states. This will allow for more efficient missile defenses and could lead to greater security cooperation in the region." Then Secretary of State Clinton continued to press the issue at the second ministerial of the U.S.-GCC Strategic Cooperation Forum on September 28, 2012, held on the sidelines of the U.N. General Assembly meetings in New York. The Forum convened again on September 26, 2013, at the sidelines of the U.N. General Assembly, but the meeting focused more on regional issues than on missile defense. Secretary of Defense Hagel stressed the need for the integrated network in his early December 2013 trip to the region. On December 16, 2013, President Obama issued a Presidential Determination to allow defense sales to the GCC as a bloc – an action reportedly intended to promote the Gulf-wide integrated missile defense network.[17]

The UAE is pivotal to the U.S. effort to forge a Gulf-wide missile defense network because the UAE has ordered the Terminal High Altitude Air Defense System (THAAD), the first sale ever of that sophisticated missile defense system. A sale of THAAD equipment was first announced September 9, 2008, valued at about $7 billion. However, subsequent negotiations altered the purchase somewhat; on November 2, 2012, DSCA notified Congress of a potential sale to the UAE of additional THAAD equipment: 9 launchers, 48 missiles, and associated equipment with

---

[15] Thom Shanker. "Arms Deal with Israel and 2 Arab Nations Is Near." *New York Times*, April 19, 2013.

[16] U.S. Department of State Daily Digest Bulletin, April 12, 2012.

[17] http://www.whitehouse.gov/the-press-office/2013/12/16/presidential-determination-gulf-cooperation-council

total estimated value of $1.135 billion.[18] In September 2013, the Defense Department awarded a $3.9 billion contract to Lockheed Martin for about 300 THAAD missiles, of which about 192 would be exported to the UAE—suggesting the UAE purchase has increased since the November 2012 DSCA notification.[19] Also on November 5, 2012, DSCA announced the first sale of the THAAD to neighboring Qatar.

Among significant other recent missile defense sales to the UAE are the advanced Patriot anti-missile systems (PAC-3, up to $9 billion value, announced December 4, 2007). Also announced on September 9, 2008, were sales to UAE of vehicle mounted "Stinger" anti-aircraft systems ($737 million value).

Defense Relations with Other Nations and Alliances

In recent years, the UAE has sought to broaden its defense relationships. In 2004, the UAE joined NATO's "Istanbul Cooperation Initiative," which was launched that year by NATO as an effort to bolster bilateral security with Middle Eastern countries. The UAE has "observer" status in NATO and, in May 2011, the UAE requested to send an Ambassador to NATO under a new alliance policy approved by the organization in April 2011. The UAE appointed an Ambassador, but UAE cooperation with NATO has waned since mid-2011 as NATO and the United States wind down involvement in Afghanistan and the European Union (EU) financial crisis has placed significant burdens on NATO country budgets. Still, in October 2013 the UAE cabinet decided to open a mission to the EU.

France has become a major defense partner for the UAE. In January 2008 the UAE signed an agreement with then French President Nicolas Sarkozy to allow a French military presence. The facilities—collectively termed Camp De La Paix ("Peace Camp") were inaugurated during a visit by Sarkozy to UAE on May 27, 2009, and include (1) a 900-foot section of the Zayid Port for use by the French navy; (2) an installation at Dhafra Air Base to be used by France's air force; and (3) a barracks at an Abu Dhabi military camp that houses about 400 French military personnel. On the other hand, in October 2010, the UAE asked Canada to evacuate a UAE base, Camp Mirage, used by Canada as a staging point for its forces to deploy to Afghanistan, when Canada refused additional landing slots in Canada for Emirates Air.[20] The two countries subsequently negotiated a resolution. The UAE has already bought 380 French-made Leclerc tanks and 60 Mirage 2000 warplanes. The UAE reportedly is evaluating whether to purchase some or all of its additional combat aircraft from non-U.S. manufacturers.

Cooperation Against Terrorism and Proliferation

The UAE cooperates extensively with U.S. efforts against terrorism and proliferation in the region, although the UAE efforts suffer from some lack of capacity and experience. The United States has sought to help the UAE redress a past pattern of lax enforcement of export and border controls that enabled technology to reach Iran and terrorists to transit and make use of the UAE financial system. The relatively small sums of U.S. aid to UAE that have been provided in recent

---

[18] Defense Security Cooperation Agency transmittal No. 12-40. November 5, 2012.

[19] National Public Radio, September 23, 2013.

[20] Chase, Steven and Brent Jang. "UAE Threatens to Kick Canada Out of Covert Military Base Camp Mirage." Toronto Globe and Mail, October 8, 2010.

years were generally for programs to improve UAE performance on enforcing export control laws and on anti-terrorism. This U.S. assistance—coupled with renewed UAE focus on enacting and enforcing additional export and border control laws—appears to have alleviated at least some of the U.S. concerns on this issue. No U.S. aid to UAE is requested for FY2014.

Terrorism Issues

During the mid-1990s, some Al Qaeda activists reportedly were able to move through and spend time in the UAE.[21] Two of the September 11 hijackers were UAE nationals, and they reportedly used UAE-based financial networks in the plot. Since then, the UAE has been credited in State Department "Country Reports on Terrorism," including the one for 2012 released May 30, 2013,[22] with numerous reforms. The reports say the UAE has arrested senior Al Qaeda operatives; denounced terror attacks; improved border security; prescribed guidance for Friday prayer leaders to criticize extremist ideology; investigated suspect financial transactions; criminalized use of the Internet by terrorist groups; and strengthened its bureaucracy and legal framework to combat terrorism. Among notable successes, in early 2009, UAE security officials reportedly broke up an Al Qaeda plot to blow up targets in Dubai emirate.[23] On October 29, 2010, UAE authorities assisted in foiling an Al Qaeda in the Arabian Peninsula plot to send bombs to the United States. On December 26, 2012, the UAE stated that it had arrested members of an alleged terrorist cell plotting attacks in the United States, in an operation conducted in cooperation with Saudi Arabia. The UAE statement indicated the alleged terrorists might be part of Al Qaeda. In April 2013, UAE authorities arrested seven non-UAE Arab nationals allegedly affiliated with Al Qaeda, although some activists said the arrests were a cover for acts of repression against Islamists.

The UAE Central Bank is credited in the recent State Department terrorism reports with providing training programs to UAE financial institutions on money laundering and terrorism financing, although actions against informal financial transmittals (*hawala*) require "further vigilance." In September 2012, the FBI Legal Attache established a sub-office at the U.S. consulate in Dubai to assist with joint efforts against terrorism and terrorism financing.

On December 13-14, 2012, during a meeting of the Global Counterterrorism Forum (GCTF), the UAE-based "International Center of Excellence for Countering Violent Extremism," known as *Hedayah*, was inaugurated. The center is an institution for training, dialogue, collaboration, and research to counter violent extremism. The UAE is a founding member of the GCTF, which was formed in September 2011.

Port and Border Controls

The UAE has signed on to several U.S. efforts to prevent proliferation and terrorism. These include the Container Security Initiative Statement of Principles, aimed at screening U.S.-bound containerized cargo transiting Dubai ports. Under it, three U.S. Customs and Border Protection officers are co-located with the Dubai Customs Intelligence Unit at Port Rashid in Dubai. The

---

[21] Department of State. Office of the Coordinator for Counterterrorism. Country Reports on Terrorism 2012. May 30, 2013. Author conversations with executive branch officials, 1997-2013.

[22] "U.S. Embassy to Reopen on Saturday After UAE Threat." *Reuters*, March 26, 2004.

[23] Lake, Eli and Sarah Carter. "UAE Kept Tight Lid on Disrupted Terror Plot." *Washington Times*, September 17, 2009.

program results in about 20 ship inspections per week of U.S.-bound containers, many of them apparently originating in Iran. The UAE is a party to the Proliferation Security Initiative, the Megaports Initiative designed to prevent terrorist from using major ports to ship illicit material, and the Customs-Trade Partnership Against Terrorism. The United States and UAE are negotiating to establish a "pre-clearance facility" at the Abu Dhabi International Airport.

Export Controls

The UAE record on preventing the re-export of advanced technology, particularly to Iran, has been mixed in past years, but has improved considerably since mid-2010. Taking advantage of geographic proximity and the high volume of Iran-Dubai trade ($10 billion per year), numerous Iranian entities involved in Iran's energy sector and its WMD programs have offices in the UAE that are used to try to procure needed technology and equipment. In connection with revelations of illicit sales of nuclear technology to Iran, Libya, and North Korea by Pakistan's nuclear scientist A.Q. Khan, Dubai was named as a key transfer point for Khan's shipments of nuclear components. Two Dubai-based companies were apparently involved in transshipping components: SMB Computers and Gulf Technical Industries.[24] On April 7, 2004, the Administration sanctioned a UAE firm, Elmstone Service and Trading FZE, for allegedly selling weapons of mass destruction-related technology to Iran, under the Iran-Syria Non-Proliferation Act (P.L. 106-178). In June 2006, the Bureau of Industry and Security (BIS) released a general order imposing a license requirement on Mayrow General Trading Company and related enterprises in the UAE. This was done after Mayrow was implicated in the transhipment of electronic components and devices capable of being used to construct improvised explosive devices (IED) used in Iraq and Afghanistan.[25]

In January 2009, the Institute for Science and International Security issued a report entitled "Iranian Entities' Illicit Military Procurement Networks," published January 12, 2009. The report asserted that Iran has used UAE companies to obtain technology from U.S. suppliers, and that the components obtained have been used to construct improvised explosive devices (IEDs) shipped by Iran to militants in Iraq and Afghanistan. Other UAE companies the report alleges were involved in this network included not only Mayrow but also Majidco Micro Electronics, Micatic General Trading, and Talinx Electronics.

The UAE has enhanced its cooperation at times when U.S. officials or outside experts have questioned its performance. In February 2007 the Administration threatened to form a new category of control called "Destinations of Diversion Control" with UAE as the intended designee country. In September 2007, the FNC adopted a law strengthening export controls (April 2007). That month, the UAE government used the new law to shut down 40 foreign and UAE firms allegedly involved in dual use exports to Iran and other countries. On July 22, 2010, Deputy Assistant Secretary of State for International Security and Nonproliferation Vann Van Diepen testified before the House Foreign Affairs Committee (Subcommittee on Terrorism, Nonproliferation and Trade) that the UAE had augmented the staff of the office that implements the 2007 law. He added that the UAE's enforcement bodies—customs, law enforcement, and intelligence services—are functioning to that end.[26] A 2010 Iran sanctions law, the

---

[24] Milhollin, Gary and Kelly Motz. "Nukes 'R' US." *New York Times* op. ed. March 4, 2004.

[25] BIS, "General Order Concerning Mayrow General Trading and Related Enterprises," 71 *Federal Register* 107, June 5, 2006.

[26] Testimony of Mr. Vann Van Diepen before the House Foreign Affairs Committee. July 22, 2010.

Comprehensive Iran Sanctions, Accountability, and Divestment Act (CISADA, P.L. 111-195) created a category of countries that would be sanctioned (restrictions on dual use U.S. exports) for a determination of non-cooperation, but the improved performance of the UAE on this issue has caused this provision not to be invoked with respect to the UAE. As a possible reflection of increased UAE vigilance on this issue, in September 2012 the UAE, as well as Bahrain, impounded shipments to Iran of items that Iran purportedly sought for use in its nuclear program. As a GCC member, the UAE participates in the U.S.-GCC Counterproliferation Workshop, which met in April 2013 in Saudi Arabia.

The issue of leakage of technology has sometimes caused U.S. criticism or questioning of UAE investment deals. In December 2008, some Members of Congress called for a review by the inter-agency Committee on Foreign Investment in the United States (CFIUS) of a proposed joint venture between Advanced Micro Devices and Advanced Technology Investment Co. of Abu Dhabi for the potential for technology transfers. In February 2006, CFIUS approved the takeover by the Dubai-owned "Dubai Ports World" company of a British firm that manages six U.S. port facilities. Members of Congress, concerned that the takeover might weaken U.S. port security, opposed it in P.L. 109-234, causing the company to divest assets involved in U.S. port operations (divestment completed in late 2006 to AIG Global Investments). Little opposition was expressed to a November 2007 investment of $7.5 billion by the Abu Dhabi Investment Authority (ADIA)in Citigroup, which was then troubled by the global financial crisis.

Regional and Foreign Policy Issues

The UAE and the United States have major interests in common in the region. The following sections analyze UAE policies on these issues.

Iran

The UAE participates in virtually all U.S. efforts to counter Iranian power and capabilities. And, UAE officials have privately backed military U.S. action, if deemed necessary to set back Iran's nuclear program.[27] However, the UAE would prefer that regional tensions be resolved diplomatically, and UAE officials welcomed the November 24, 2013, interim nuclear agreement. At the same time, as noted, UAE officials are said to be concerned that a potential improvement in U.S.-Iran relations could cause the United States to reduce its commitments to the security of the Gulf. The UAE would also benefit economically from a reduction of sanctions on Iran and a corresponding rebound in UAE-Iran trade. Much of the trade between the two consists of re-exportation of U.S. and European goods to Iran. Since 2010, when international sanctions on Iran began tightening dramatically, UAE-Iran trade has dropped from $23 billion annually to about $4 billion, a decline that has economically harmed the powerful UAE trading community.

In addition to concerns about Iran's nuclear program, UAE officials, particularly Abu Dhabi, have long asserted that the large Iranian-origin community in Dubai emirate (estimated at 400,000 persons) could pose a "fifth column" threat to UAE stability. This large population of Iranian expatriates is a product of long-standing UAE-Iran commercial ties; many Iranian firms and individuals—primarily in the import-export business—operate from the UAE, taking advantage of the UAE's drive to position itself as a global trading and financial hub. At the same time, the

---

[27] Author conversations with UAE officials. 2009-2013.

UAE seeks to deny Iran any justification for aggression or adverse action against the UAE, and it allowed then Iranian President Mahmoud Ahmadinejad to hold a rally for Iranian expatriates in Dubai in May 2007. Reflecting the underlying tensions of UAE-Iran relations, the two countries issued mutual recriminations in January 2009 over the UAE decision in late 2008 to begin fingerprinting Iranian visitors to UAE.

The extensive Iranian commercial presence in the UAE also gives the United States ample opportunity to enlist the UAE in a multilateral effort to stiffen international sanctions on Iran. In October 2010, the UAE government directed its banks to fully comply with the restrictions outlined in U.N. Security Council Resolution 1929 (adopted June 9, 2010). In February 2012, the Noor Islamic Bank in Dubai, which Iran used to process much of its receipts of hard currency for its oil sales internationally,[28] announced it would no longer handle transactions with Iranian banks. UAE representatives say that Iranian-owned banks that continue to operate in UAE, including Bank Saderat and Bank Melli, do so only in cash and are relatively inactive. Closing them outright would, according to UAE officials, unduly antagonize Iran.

The UAE and other Gulf oil producers have cooperated with U.S. efforts to reduce Iran's oil income by offering to sell more oil to countries that want to reduce their buys from Iran. Still, some small firms in the UAE continue to supply gasoline to Iran even though such activity is potentially sanctionable under the Iran Sanctions Act (P.L. 104-172, as amended). Some UAE firms have been sanctioned under the act for those sales.

Gulf Islands Dispute

Iranian actions against the UAE in the Gulf have contributed to the UAE's strategic closeness to the United States. In April 1992, Iran asserted complete control of the largely uninhabited Persian Gulf island of Abu Musa, which it and the UAE shared under a 1971 bilateral agreement. (In 1971, Iran, then ruled by the U.S.-backed Shah, seized two other islands, Greater and Lesser Tunb, from the emirate of Ras al-Khaymah, as well as part of Abu Musa from the emirate of Sharjah.) The UAE has called for peaceful resolution of the issue through direct negotiations, referral to the International Court of Justice, or through another agreed forum. The U.S. position is that it takes no position on the sovereignty of the islands, but it supports the UAE's call to negotiate the dispute.

In October 2008—two months after the UAE protested Iran's opening in August 2008 of administrative and maritime security offices on Abu Musa—the UAE and Iran signed an agreement to establish a joint commission to resolve the dispute. Iran later allowed Sharjah to open power and water desalination facilities on the island. But, the dispute inflamed again on April 11, 2012, when then Iranian President Mahmoud Ahmadinejad visited Abu Musa and spoke to the inhabitants there, mostly Iranian fishermen. The UAE withdrew its ambassador from Tehran, and UAE officials said the action undermined many months of quiet UAE-Iran diplomacy on the issue, including the naming of negotiators on both sides. Iran further antagonized the UAE on the issue with a May 2, 2012, visit to the island by Islamic Revolutionary Guard Corps (IRGC) Commander-in-Chief Mohammad Ali Jafari, accompanied by several Iranian parliamentarians, to discuss making the island a tourist hub. In his September 28, 2013, speech to the U.N. General Assembly, the UAE Foreign Minister demanded an end to

---

[28] Alan Cowell. "Dubai Bank Reduces Ties With Iran, It Reports." *New York Times*, March 1, 2012.

Iran's "continued occupation" of the islands and called on the international community to prod Iran to settle the issue.

The November 24, 2013, interim nuclear agreement, by lowering Iran-Gulf tensions, might provide prospects to resolve the issue. UAE Foreign Minister Abdullah bin Zayid al-Nuhayyan visited Tehran on November 28, 2013, and obtained an agreement from Iran to begin bilateral discussions on the status of Abu Musa. Iran also reportedly began reducing its presence on the island. On December 4, 2013, Iranian Foreign Minister Mohammad Javad Zarif visited UAE and obtained an agreement in principle from President Khalifa to visit Iran in the near future. Experts say the two countries are discussing a possible solution under which Iran might cede control of the disputed islands in exchange for rights to the seabed around them.[29]

Iraq

Aside from allowing U.S. use of UAE military facilities during the U.S. military intervention in Iraq in 2003, the UAE has undertaken several initiatives to support U.S. efforts to stabilize Iraq since the fall of Saddam Hussein. During 2003-2011, when international forces were helping secure Iraq, the UAE provided facilities for Germany to train Iraqi police. Agreeing with the U.S. view that Sunni Arab states need to engage the Shiite-dominated government in Baghdad, in June 2008, the UAE appointed an Ambassador to Iraq, Abdullah Ibrahim al-Shehi, the first Arab country to do so. Abu Dhabi Crown Prince Shaykh Mohammad bin Zayid visited Iraq in October 2008. In October 2011, the UAE announced it intends to open a consulate in the Kurdish region of Iraq which comprises three northern provinces and is administered by the Kurdistan Regional Government (KRG), a legally constituted region within Iraq. The consulate has not opened, to date.

In humanitarian efforts, the UAE provided about $215 million for Iraq reconstruction in the form of humanitarian contributions. Some of the funds have been used to rebuild hospitals in Iraq and to provide medical treatment to Iraqi children in the UAE. Bilateral trade is estimated at about $5 billion, and UAE companies reportedly are investing in housing and other projects in Iraq. In July 2008, the UAE wrote off $7 billion (including interest) in Iraqi debt.

Afghanistan and Pakistan

The UAE was one of only three countries (Pakistan and Saudi Arabia were the others) to have recognized the Taliban during 1996-2001 as the government of Afghanistan, even though the Taliban regime was harboring Osama bin Laden and other Al Qaeda leaders. During Taliban rule, the UAE allowed Ariana Afghan airlines to operate direct service between the two countries. After the September 11, 2001, attacks, the UAE helped the United States oust the Taliban regime from Afghanistan by making available its military facilities for U.S. and allied use, as discussed. The UAE continues to assist the U.S. and international mission to stabilize Afghanistan with a 250-person contingent of UAE troops serving in Afghanistan since 2003. The UAE forces, the only Arab combat forces in Afghanistan, operate in the restive southern part of Afghanistan, particularly Uruzgan Province, where they have been welcomed by the population. UAE representatives say that UAE forces will remain in Afghanistan alongside any U.S. forces that remain after the end of the current international security mission in 2014. The UAE has a

---

[29] Awad Mustafa. "Iran, UAE Close to Deal on Hormuz Islands." *Defense News*, December 9, 2013.

counterpart to the Obama Administration's Special Representative for Afghanistan and Pakistan (SRAP).

The UAE has provided about $350 million in economic aid for Afghanistan since the fall of the Taliban. Among the projects funded with UAE aid include "Zayed University," a college serving over 6,000 Afghan students per year; six medical clinics; a major hospital with a capacity of 7,000 patients; the building of "Zayed City" that houses 200 Afghan families displaced by violence; 160 drinking wells; and 38 mosques.[30]

In related aid for U.S. regional policy, the UAE has provided over $800 million to Pakistan since 2001. Abu Dhabi hosted the November 2008 meeting of the "Friends of Pakistan" donors group that jointly helped Pakistan through its financial difficulties. As part of its assistance to Pakistan, the UAE provided about $100 million to aid victims of a major earthquake in Pakistan in October 2005, and about $20 million in 2011 to help victims of flooding there.

"Arab Spring" Issues

The UAE has joined its GCC allies in attempting to keep uprisings elsewhere in the Arab world from affecting the GCC countries themselves and to support the accession of friendly regimes in Arab states that have undergone major political change. As an indication of how the U.S. dialogue with the UAE and the GCC more broadly is evolving, the communique of the September 26, 2013, U.S.-GCC Strategic Cooperation Forum focused extensively on issues related to the Arab uprisings. To exercise leverage and influence, the UAE has used primarily—although not exclusively—its financial wherewithal.

Bahrain

Within the GCC—a core UAE concern—the UAE joined other GCC states in supporting the Al Khalifa regime in Bahrain against the 2011 uprising. The UAE sent 500 UAE police to join a 1,000 troop Saudi force that deployed to Bahrain during March-June 2011. The UAE, Saudi Arabia, Kuwait, and Qatar also have provided financial help to Bahrain and Oman; Oman faced significant protests in 2011. The G-8 countries have set up a "Transition Fund" to help Bahrain, Oman, and other Arab countries experiencing unrest, and the UAE pledged $5 million to the fund in May 2013.

Assisting Armed Rebellions: Libya and Syria

To promote political change that the UAE supports, the UAE has assisted the rebel movements in Libya and Syria, although to different extents in the two cases. In Libya, UAE supported helped the opposition to Muammar Qadhafi succeed in ending his regime in late August 2011. During that conflict, the UAE sent six (a squadron) of its U.S-made F-16s and six Mirage fighters (a squadron) to participate in the NATO-led no-fly zone enforcement and ground target strike operations in Libya. It reportedly sent some weapons to the Libyan rebels, although U.S. officials denied a UAE request to send the rebels U.S.-supplied weaponry.[31] On May 10, 2011, Abu Dhabi

---

[30] Information provided to CRS by the UAE Embassy in Washington, DC, December 2009.

[31] James Risen, Mark Mazzetti, and Michael Schmidt. "Militant Forces Got Arms Meant for Libya Rebels." *New York Times*, December 6, 2012.

hosted a major meeting of Libyan dissidents, including representatives of cities and towns still under Qadhafi regime control. In June 2011, the UAE formally recognized the Benghazi-based Transitional National Council (TNC) as the sole representative of the Libyan people and pledged financial support to it. In March 2012, the UAE transferred 58 aging Mirage 2000 combat aircraft to the fledgling post-Qadhafi government. The UAE has provided about $13 million in aid to post-Qadhafi Libya through the UAE government and UAE charity organizations.

In Syria, as the regime intensified a crackdown against a peaceful uprising that began in March 2011, the UAE and the other GCC states leaders shifted decisively against Assad, at least in part to strategically weaken Iran in the Middle East. In November 2011, after the Arab League suspended Syria's membership, the UAE embassy in Damascus, among others, was attacked. It closed that embassy, as the other GCC states did theirs, in February 2012. The UAE joined its GCC allies in early April 2012, during a multinational conference on Syria in Istanbul, in offering about $100 million in funds to Syrian rebels, to be used as salaries and also presumably to buy weapons and services useful to their cause. However, in contrast to Saudi Arabia and Qatar, the UAE is not reported to be supplying weapons to the Syrian rebels. The UAE and its GCC allies also have had differences over which rebel groups to assist; the UAE tends to oppose aid to Syrian rebels linked to the Muslim Brotherhood. The UAE also has sought greater U.S. involvement in Syria crisis; in June 2013 the UAE declined to host a meeting of allied defense officials on Syria, maintaining that the meeting would be unproductive without extensive U.S. participation on the Syria issue.[32] In concert with its GCC partners, the UAE has taken steps to punish Gulf-based supporters of Lebanese Hezbollah for Hezbollah's military support to Assad.

In providing humanitarian aid to alleviate suffering from the Syria crisis, the UAE Embassy in Washington, DC, said that, as of March 2013, the UAE government and various UAE charity organizations (Red Crescent Authority, Khalifa bin Zayid Al Nuhayyan Foundation, and Sharjah Chairty Association) had donated at least $330 million to help Syrian refugees. The UAE separately has given $1.25 billion to Jordan to help it cope with the Syrian refugees that have fled there because of the violence. And, UAE forces are participating in the June 2013 "Eager Lion" military exercises in Jordan intended to insulate Jordan from any Syria conflict spillover. The UAE also has given economic aid to Lebanon, perhaps in part to counter Iranian and Syrian influence there—an objective that UAE shares with Saudi Arabia and the other GCC states.

Yemen

In Yemen, the UAE joined a high-profile GCC mediation effort that reached an agreement for President Ali Abdullah Saleh to step down in favor of a political transition. President Saleh was injured in an assassination attempt in June 2011 and recuperated in Saudi Arabia, but he returned to the country in November 2011. He later signed the transition agreement and left office on January 22, 2012.

Egypt

The UAE has also aligned with some of the other Gulf states in attempting to build a post-Mubarak political structure in Egypt that is friendly to the UAE. The UAE, as noted above, has

---

[32] Mark Mazzetti, Michael Gordon, and Mark Landler. "U.S. Is Said to Plan to Send Weapons to Syrian Rebels." *New York Times*, June 14, 2013.

arrested domestic supporters of the Muslim Brotherhood, and the UAE was displeased by the 2012 election of a leader of the Muslim Brotherhood, Mohammad Morsi, as President. The UAE was therefore supportive of the Egyptian military's ouster of Morsi in early July 2013. Within a week of Morsi's ouster, the UAE backed a Saudi effort to financially stabilize the military-led government in Cairo. The UAE pledged $3 billion in assistance as part of the broader Saudi-led package totaling $12 billion ($5 billion from Saudi Arabia and $4 billion from Kuwait, in addition to the UAE funds).

Arab-Israeli Dispute

On the Arab-Israeli issue, the UAE wants to ensure that any settlement between Israel and the Palestinians is "just," meaning sufficiently beneficial to the Palestinians. It has sometimes criticized the United States as excessively supportive of Israel, although it generally expresses that criticism in private meetings with U.S officials. UAE leaders publicly backed the Palestinian Authority's bid for statehood recognition at the United Nations General Assembly in September 2011—a proposal the United States opposed as premature and preemptive of Israeli-Palestinian negotiations. In December 2008 and January 2009, the UAE government permitted street demonstrations in support of Hamas during its war with Israel. In February 2009, the UAE denied a visa to an Israeli tennis player who was to participate in a Dubai tennis tournament, earning the UAE some international criticism. It also aggressively investigated and, based on evidence developed, formally accused Israel in the killing of a Hamas leader in Dubai in January 2010.

The UAE has not advanced its own far-reaching proposals to resolve the Israeli-Palestinian dispute, as has King Abdullah of Saudi Arabia. Nor has UAE tried to directly mediate between Palestinian factions, as have Saudi Arabia, Qatar, or Egypt. In 1994 the UAE joined with the other Gulf monarchies in ending enforcement of the Arab League's boycott of companies doing business with Israel and on companies that deal with companies that do business with Israel. The UAE formally bans direct trade with Israel, although UAE companies reportedly do business with Israeli firms and some Israeli diplomats have attended multilateral meetings in the UAE. Unlike Qatar and Oman, the UAE did not host multilateral Arab-Israeli working groups on regional issues when those talks took place during 1994-1998. In 2007, the UAE joined a "quartet" of Arab states (the others are Saudi Arabia, Egypt, and Jordan) to assist U.S. diplomacy on Israeli-Palestinian issues, and it attended the Annapolis summit on the issue that year.

The UAE has sometimes put its considerable financial resources to work on behalf of the Palestinians. According to the UAE government, the UAE has provided nearly $550 million to humanitarian projects for Palestinian refugees in the Palestinian territories, and in Syria; the funds have been channeled in part through the U.N. Relief Works Agency (UNRWA). One major UAE action has been to fund a housing project in Rafah, in the Gaza Strip, called "Shaykh Khalifa City."

Other UAE Foreign Aid[33]

The UAE asserts that it has provided billions of dollars in international aid through its government and through funds controlled by royal family members and other elites, aside from

---

[33] Factsheet provided by UAE Embassy in Washington, DC, June 2011.

funds provided for the specific crises discussed above. Among initiatives outside the Near East and South Asia region:

- In 2012, the UAE, through the government and UAE-based relief groups, spent $1.5 billion in foreign aid worldwide, of which $600 million went to mainly Jordan, the Palestinian territories, Yemen, and Azerbaijan. One fund, the Abu Dhabi Fund for Development (ADFD), established in 1971, has distributed about $3.5 billion to 207 projects in 53 countries. Of this amount, about $240 million was distributed in 2010.

- The UAE provided $100 million to aid victims of the December 2004 tsunami in the Indian Ocean.

- In May 2011, the UAE donated $30 million to the Australian state of Queensland to fund cyclone shelters.

- In July 2011, UAE foundations responded to a U.N. appeal for aid to the victims of a drought in East Africa.

- In February 2012, the UAE announced an additional $2 million donation to the Local Stability Fund that provides relief to victims of conflict in Somalia. In October 2013, the UAE cabinet decided to reopen a UAE embassy in Mogadishu, in part to facilitate the delivery of relief to Somalis.

- The UAE has donated substantial sums for humanitarian causes in the United States, including $150 million for a cancer center at the University of Texas; $100 million to assist New Orleans after Hurricane Katrina in 2005; $150 million to a children's medical center in Washington, DC, in 2009; and $1 million worth of Apple laptop computers to the Joplin, Missouri, public schools systems in the wake of the May 2011 tornado there.

Nuclear Agreement[34]

The government of the United Arab Emirates (UAE) announced in 2008 an ambitious plan to acquire its first nuclear power reactors to satisfy projected increases in domestic electricity demand.[35] The United States and the UAE signed an agreement on January 15, 2009, to help the UAE develop a nuclear power program. However, some in Congress expressed concerns about this agreement because of fears of potential leakage of technology to Iran as well as the potential for additional regional proliferation of nuclear technology.

Policymakers and advisers in the government of Abu Dhabi, in consultation with representatives from the other six emirates, are guiding the program's implementation. A number of U.S. and European firms have secured administrative and financial advisory contracts with the program. The agreement for the United States to assist the program, subject to conditions specified in

---

[34] This section was prepared by Paul Kerr, Analyst in Weapons of Mass Destruction Nonproliferation, CRS. See CRS Report R40344, *The United Arab Emirates Nuclear Program and Proposed U.S. Nuclear Cooperation*, by Christopher M. Blanchard and Paul K. Kerr.

[35] UAE officials estimate that their country must expand its power generation and transmission capacity from the current level of 16 gigawatts to 40 gigawatts by 2020 in order to meet projected demand increases

Section 123 of the Atomic Energy Act of 1954 [42 U.S.C. 2153(b)], was signed by the Obama Administration on May 21, 2009 (and submitted to Congress that day). It became effective when Congress declined to block the arrangement within 90 days of continuous legislative session following the May 21 submission. Several congressional resolutions of approval of the agreement (S.J.Res. 18 and H.J.Res. 60) were introduced, compared to only one disapproving (H.J.Res. 55). No measure blocking the agreement was enacted, and the "1-2-3 Agreement" entered into force on December 17, 2009. Nor was an earlier bill in the 111th Congress, H.R. 364, requiring the President to certify that the UAE has taken a number of steps to stop illicit trade with Iran before any agreement would take effect, enacted into law.

In January 2010, the UAE announced that it had chosen the Korea Electric Power Corporation (KEPCO of South Korea) to construct the first of four APR1400 nuclear reactors that would sell electricity to the Abu Dhabi Water and Electricity Authority. The first plant is expected to start operating in 2017 and the other three are scheduled to be completed and operational by 2020, according to the UAE.[36] The plant construction is to take place at Baraka, near Abu Dhabi's western border with Saudi Arabia, pending final approval by the UAE Federal Authority for Nuclear Regulation.[37]

The Emirates Nuclear Energy Corporation (ENEC) announced in July 2011 that it has begun a "procurement competition" to obtain fuel supplies for the four proposed reactors.[38] "The final contracts are expected to be signed in the first quarter of 2012," according to the ENEC. No specific decisions have been made regarding the disposition of spent reactor fuel. The UAE has committed to refrain from domestic uranium enrichment and reprocessing spent nuclear reactor fuel. Enrichment and reprocessing are considered to the most sensitive parts of the nuclear fuel cycle because they can both produce fissile material for nuclear weapons.

The International Atomic Energy Agency announced December 14, 2011, that a group of experts had completed a review of the UAE's "regulatory framework for nuclear safety and radiation protection." Providing further reassurances to U.S. officials, the review both "noted good practices" and provided suggestions to the Federal Authority for Nuclear Regulation, the UAE's nuclear regulatory authority.[39]

Economic Issues

The UAE, a member of the World Trade Organization (WTO), has developed a free market economy, but one that is widely considered weakly regulated. Partly as a result, the UAE, particularly Dubai emirate, pursued economic strategies built on attracting investment to construct large numbers of opulent and futuristic projects designed to attract expatriates and international tourists. The UAE is participating in Gulf-wide economic infrastructure projects such as a railroad network connecting all the GCC states, to become operational by 2017.

---

[36] http://enec.gov.ae/our-nuclear-energy-program/prime-contractor/.

[37] http://enec.gov.ae/our-nuclear-energy-program/preferred-site/.

[38] http://www.enec.gov.ae/media-centre/news/content/emirates-nuclear-energy-corporation-begins-nuclear-fuel-procurement-co.

[39] http://www.iaea.org/press/?p=2572.

The UAE economy was affected significantly by the 2007-2009 global financial crisis, which caused widespread layoffs in UAE and the departure of thousands of foreign workers, and left UAE banks with vast amounts of nonperforming loans.[40] The downturn in real estate prices also affected regional investors, such as those in Afghanistan, who bought into high-end housing such as on the Palm Islands. The fall in value nearly caused a collapse of a major Afghan bank, Kabul Bank, in September 2010.

To address the crisis, the federal government took on some public debt and drew upon some of the country's purported $700 billion invested in "sovereign wealth funds" to inject into Dubai banks to help them ride out the downturn. The largest such fund, called Mubadala, is owned and run by Abu Dhabi. However, by the end of 2011, the UAE's worst economic problems were behind it and its growth improved substantially to about 3.3% for all of 2011. Growth was about 4% for 2013, according to the IMF.

Oil and Gas Sector/Dedication to Future Clean Energy

The source of the UAE's sovereign wealth has been oil sales. Abu Dhabi has 80% of the federation's proven oil reserves of about 100 billion barrels, enough for over 100 years of exports at the current production rate of about 2.5 million–2.7 million barrels per day (mbd). Of that, over 2 mbd are exported, and the UAE may have as much as 500,000 bpd of spare capacity.[41] Small amounts of its oil exports go to the United States, while the largest share of UAE oil goes to Japan. The UAE has vast quantities of natural gas but consumes more than it produces. It has entered into a deal (Dolphin project) with neighboring countries under which a recently constructed pipeline carries natural gas from the large gas exporter, Qatar, to the UAE and on to Oman as well.

In addition, the UAE is trying to secure its oil export routes against any threat by Iran to close the strategic Strait of Hormuz, through with the UAE and other major oil exporters transport their oil exports. In mid-July 2012, the UAE loaded its first tanker of oil following completion of the Abu Dhabi Crude Oil Pipeline (ADCOP) which terminates in the emirate of Fujairah, on the Gulf of Oman. The line, which cost $3 billion, has a capacity to transport 1.5 million barrels per day of crude oil—about half of the UAE's peak production. The UAE is also planning a large refinery near that terminal, and possibly a second oil pipeline exiting there, to further secure its oil exports and value-added petroleum products.[42]

Seeking to reinvest its oil wealth, Abu Dhabi has sought in recent years to outdo Dubai by building local branches of famous U.S. and European museums. However, it has also tried to use its oil wealth to plan for a time when the developed world is no longer reliant on oil imports. It has funded "Masdar City"—a project, the first phase of which is to be completed in 2015, to build a planned city which will rely only on renewable energy sources. Automobiles that run on fossil fuels are banned from Masdar City. One feature of the city is a system of driverless taxis that use automation to take passengers to their destinations. The civilian nuclear energy project discussed above is also part of the effort to plan for a post-oil world economy.

---

[40] Worth, Robert. "Laid Off Foreigners Flee as Dubai Spirals Down." *New York Times*, February 12, 2008.

[41] http://www.thenational.ae/events/areas/abu-dhabi/adnoc-preserves-spare-supplies.

[42] "Abu Dhabi: In the Pipeline." The Middle East, January 26, 2012.

U.S.-UAE Trade and Trade Promotion Discussions

U.S. trade with the UAE is a significant issue because the UAE is the largest market for U.S. exports to the Middle East. In 2012, U.S. firms exported nearly $22 billion worth of goods to the UAE. Over 1,000 U.S. companies have offices there and there are 60,000 Americans working in UAE. U.S. exports to UAE in coming years (2014-2018) are expected to be very large because of a spate of orders for U.S. commercial aircraft in 2013 by expanding UAE airlines Emirates Air and Ettihad Airlines. Many of these orders were placed at the Dubai Air Show in November 2013.

On November 15, 2004, the Administration notified Congress it had begun negotiating a free trade agreement (FTA) with the UAE. Several rounds of talks were held prior to the June 2007 expiration of Administration "trade promotion authority," but progress was halting. The FTA talks have been replaced by an U.S.-UAE "Economic Policy Dialogue, involving the major U.S. economic departments and their UAE counterparts. The dialogue, consisting of two meetings per year, began in late 2011 and also included discussion of reform of UAE export controls, an issue discussed above. In addition, as part of the GCC, the UAE is negotiating with the United States a "GCC-U.S. Framework Agreement on Trade, Economic, Investment, and Technical Cooperation," an umbrella instrument for promoting ties between the two sides in the economic area—essentially a GCC-wide trade and investment framework agreement (TIFA). The negotiations were led by the U.S. Trade Representative (USTR), and an agreement was signed on September 25, 2012.

The UAE, which is considered wealthy, has received small amounts of U.S. assistance. The primary purpose of the aid is to make the UAE eligible for advice and programming to improve its border security and export controls, as shown below. None is requested for FY2014.

Table 2. Recent U.S. Aid to UAE

(in thousands of dollars)

	FY07	FY08	FY09	FY10	FY11	FY12	FY13	FY14 (req)
NADR (Nonproliferation, Anti-Terrorism, Demining, and Related)— Counterterrorism Programs (ATA)	1,409		725					
NADR-Combating WMD	172	300	200	230	230			
International Military Education and Training (IMET)				10				
Totals	**1,581**	**300**	**925**	**240**	**230**	**0**	**0**	**0**

Author Contact Information

Kenneth Katzman
Specialist in Middle Eastern Affairs
kkatzman@crs.loc.gov, 7-7612

www.ingramcontent.com/pod-product-compliance
Lightning Source LLC
Chambersburg PA
CBHW080748290526
45790CB00008B/3370